50 Savory Slow Cooker Meals for Busy Days

By: Kelly Johnson

Table of Contents

- Beef Stew with Vegetables
- Chicken Tikka Masala
- Pulled Pork Sandwiches
- Vegetable Chili
- Beef and Broccoli Stir-Fry
- Honey Garlic Chicken
- White Bean and Ham Soup
- Creamy Tomato Basil Soup
- Cajun Chicken and Sausage Gumbo
- Sweet and Sour Meatballs
- Slow Cooker Ribs with Barbecue Sauce
- Chicken and Dumplings
- Beef Stroganoff
- Mediterranean Chickpea Stew
- Classic Beef Chili
- Teriyaki Chicken with Pineapple
- Savory Pot Roast with Potatoes
- Lemon Garlic Herb Chicken
- Stuffed Bell Peppers
- Beef and Mushroom Stroganoff
- Thai Red Curry with Chicken
- Moroccan Lamb Tagine
- Chicken Enchilada Casserole
- Lentil and Spinach Soup
- Garlic Parmesan Chicken Wings
- BBQ Brisket
- Curried Lentil Stew
- Shrimp and Grits
- Chicken Fajitas
- Italian Sausage and Peppers
- Chicken and Rice Casserole
- Classic French Onion Soup
- Jambalaya with Chicken and Sausage
- Beef and Vegetable Stir-Fry
- Creamy Mushroom Chicken

- Stuffed Cabbage Rolls
- Spanish Chicken and Rice
- Italian Meatball Soup
- Zesty Ranch Chicken
- Vegetable and Quinoa Chili
- Coconut Curry Chicken
- Pork Carnitas
- Chicken Cacciatore
- BBQ Chicken Thighs
- Beef Bourguignon
- Chicken Tortilla Soup
- Tomato and Basil Risotto
- Beef and Barley Soup
- Italian Sausage and Lentil Soup
- Chicken Parmesan Pasta

Beef Stew with Vegetables

Ingredients:

- 2 pounds beef chuck, cut into 1-inch cubes
- 3 tablespoons olive oil
- 1 onion, chopped
- 3 carrots, sliced
- 3 potatoes, diced
- 3 cloves garlic, minced
- 4 cups beef broth
- 2 tablespoons tomato paste
- 2 teaspoons dried thyme
- 2 bay leaves
- Salt and pepper to taste
- Fresh parsley for garnish

Instructions:

1. **Brown the Beef:** In a large pot, heat olive oil over medium-high heat. Add the beef cubes and brown on all sides. Remove and set aside.
2. **Sauté Vegetables:** In the same pot, add onion and garlic. Sauté until softened. Add carrots and potatoes.
3. **Add Remaining Ingredients:** Return the beef to the pot. Stir in beef broth, tomato paste, thyme, bay leaves, salt, and pepper.
4. **Simmer:** Bring to a boil, then reduce heat to low. Cover and simmer for 1.5 to 2 hours, or until beef is tender.
5. **Serve:** Remove bay leaves, garnish with parsley, and serve hot.

Chicken Tikka Masala

Ingredients:

- 1 pound boneless, skinless chicken thighs, cut into bite-sized pieces
- 1 cup plain yogurt
- 2 tablespoons garam masala
- 1 tablespoon turmeric
- 1 tablespoon cumin
- 1 tablespoon paprika
- 2 tablespoons olive oil
- 1 onion, chopped
- 3 cloves garlic, minced
- 1 can (14 oz) crushed tomatoes
- 1 cup heavy cream
- Salt and pepper to taste
- Fresh cilantro for garnish

Instructions:

1. **Marinate Chicken:** In a bowl, combine yogurt, garam masala, turmeric, cumin, and paprika. Add chicken and coat well. Marinate for at least 30 minutes or overnight.
2. **Cook Chicken:** In a large skillet, heat olive oil over medium-high heat. Add marinated chicken and cook until browned. Remove and set aside.
3. **Sauté Onion and Garlic:** In the same skillet, add onion and garlic. Sauté until softened.
4. **Add Tomatoes and Cream:** Stir in crushed tomatoes, salt, and pepper. Cook for 5 minutes, then add heavy cream and bring to a simmer.
5. **Combine:** Return chicken to the skillet and simmer for 10 minutes until heated through.
6. **Serve:** Garnish with fresh cilantro and serve with rice or naan.

Pulled Pork Sandwiches

Ingredients:

- 3 pounds pork shoulder
- 1 tablespoon paprika
- 1 tablespoon brown sugar
- 1 tablespoon garlic powder
- 1 tablespoon onion powder
- 1 teaspoon cayenne pepper
- Salt and pepper to taste
- 1 cup barbecue sauce
- Burger buns for serving
- Coleslaw for topping (optional)

Instructions:

1. **Season Pork:** In a small bowl, mix paprika, brown sugar, garlic powder, onion powder, cayenne pepper, salt, and pepper. Rub the mixture all over the pork shoulder.
2. **Cook Pork:** Place the pork in a slow cooker and cook on low for 8 hours or until tender and easily shredded.
3. **Shred Pork:** Once cooked, remove the pork from the slow cooker and shred with two forks. Stir in barbecue sauce.
4. **Serve:** Serve on burger buns topped with coleslaw if desired.

Vegetable Chili

Ingredients:

- 1 tablespoon olive oil
- 1 onion, chopped
- 2 cloves garlic, minced
- 1 bell pepper, chopped
- 2 carrots, diced
- 1 zucchini, diced
- 1 can (14 oz) diced tomatoes
- 1 can (15 oz) kidney beans, drained and rinsed
- 1 can (15 oz) black beans, drained and rinsed
- 2 cups vegetable broth
- 2 tablespoons chili powder
- 1 teaspoon cumin
- Salt and pepper to taste
- Fresh cilantro for garnish

Instructions:

1. **Sauté Vegetables:** In a large pot, heat olive oil over medium heat. Add onion and garlic, sauté until softened. Add bell pepper, carrots, and zucchini, cooking for another 5 minutes.
2. **Add Remaining Ingredients:** Stir in diced tomatoes, kidney beans, black beans, vegetable broth, chili powder, cumin, salt, and pepper.
3. **Simmer:** Bring to a boil, then reduce heat to low. Cover and simmer for 20-30 minutes, stirring occasionally.
4. **Serve:** Garnish with fresh cilantro and serve hot.

Beef and Broccoli Stir-Fry

Ingredients:

- 1 pound beef sirloin, sliced thinly
- 2 cups broccoli florets
- 2 tablespoons soy sauce
- 2 tablespoons oyster sauce
- 1 tablespoon cornstarch
- 2 tablespoons vegetable oil
- 2 cloves garlic, minced
- Cooked rice for serving

Instructions:

1. **Marinate Beef:** In a bowl, mix sliced beef with soy sauce, oyster sauce, and cornstarch. Let it marinate for 15 minutes.
2. **Cook Broccoli:** In a large skillet, heat 1 tablespoon of vegetable oil over medium heat. Add broccoli and stir-fry for 3-4 minutes until bright green and tender. Remove and set aside.
3. **Stir-Fry Beef:** In the same skillet, add the remaining oil. Add garlic and marinated beef, stir-frying until browned and cooked through.
4. **Combine:** Return broccoli to the skillet and toss to combine.
5. **Serve:** Serve hot over cooked rice.

Honey Garlic Chicken

Ingredients:

- 1 pound boneless, skinless chicken thighs
- 1/4 cup honey
- 1/4 cup soy sauce
- 3 cloves garlic, minced
- 1 tablespoon olive oil
- Salt and pepper to taste
- Sesame seeds for garnish (optional)
- Chopped green onions for garnish (optional)

Instructions:

1. **Make Sauce:** In a bowl, whisk together honey, soy sauce, and garlic.
2. **Cook Chicken:** In a skillet, heat olive oil over medium-high heat. Season chicken thighs with salt and pepper. Cook for 5-6 minutes on each side until golden and cooked through.
3. **Add Sauce:** Pour the honey garlic sauce over the chicken and simmer for an additional 2-3 minutes, coating the chicken.
4. **Serve:** Garnish with sesame seeds and green onions, and serve hot.

White Bean and Ham Soup

Ingredients:

- 1 tablespoon olive oil
- 1 onion, chopped
- 2 cloves garlic, minced
- 2 carrots, diced
- 2 celery stalks, diced
- 4 cups chicken broth
- 2 cans (15 oz each) white beans, drained and rinsed
- 2 cups diced ham
- 1 teaspoon thyme
- Salt and pepper to taste
- Fresh parsley for garnish

Instructions:

1. **Sauté Vegetables:** In a large pot, heat olive oil over medium heat. Add onion, garlic, carrots, and celery, cooking until softened.
2. **Add Remaining Ingredients:** Stir in chicken broth, white beans, ham, thyme, salt, and pepper.
3. **Simmer:** Bring to a boil, then reduce heat to low and simmer for 20-30 minutes.
4. **Serve:** Garnish with fresh parsley and serve hot.

Creamy Tomato Basil Soup

Ingredients:

- 2 tablespoons olive oil
- 1 onion, chopped
- 3 cloves garlic, minced
- 1 can (28 oz) crushed tomatoes
- 2 cups vegetable broth
- 1 cup heavy cream
- 1/4 cup fresh basil, chopped
- Salt and pepper to taste

Instructions:

1. **Sauté Onion and Garlic:** In a large pot, heat olive oil over medium heat. Add onion and garlic, sautéing until softened.
2. **Add Tomatoes and Broth:** Stir in crushed tomatoes and vegetable broth. Bring to a boil, then reduce heat and simmer for 15 minutes.
3. **Blend Soup:** Use an immersion blender to puree the soup until smooth. Stir in heavy cream, basil, salt, and pepper.
4. **Serve:** Serve hot, garnished with additional basil if desired.

Enjoy cooking these hearty and flavorful dishes!

Cajun Chicken and Sausage Gumbo

Ingredients:

- 1 pound andouille sausage, sliced
- 1 pound boneless, skinless chicken thighs, diced
- 1/2 cup vegetable oil
- 1/2 cup all-purpose flour
- 1 onion, chopped
- 1 bell pepper, chopped
- 2 celery stalks, chopped
- 4 cloves garlic, minced
- 6 cups chicken broth
- 1 can (14.5 oz) diced tomatoes
- 2 cups okra, sliced
- 2 tablespoons Cajun seasoning
- Salt and pepper to taste
- 2 bay leaves
- Cooked rice for serving
- Chopped green onions for garnish

Instructions:

1. **Make the Roux:** In a large pot, heat vegetable oil over medium heat. Stir in flour, cooking and stirring continuously until the mixture is dark brown, about 15-20 minutes.
2. **Add Vegetables:** Add onion, bell pepper, celery, and garlic to the roux. Cook until vegetables are tender.
3. **Add Meats and Broth:** Stir in sausage and chicken, cooking until browned. Add chicken broth, diced tomatoes, okra, Cajun seasoning, salt, pepper, and bay leaves. Bring to a boil.
4. **Simmer:** Reduce heat and simmer for 45 minutes, stirring occasionally.
5. **Serve:** Remove bay leaves, serve over cooked rice, and garnish with green onions.

Sweet and Sour Meatballs

Ingredients:

- 1 pound ground beef
- 1/2 cup breadcrumbs
- 1/4 cup onion, finely chopped
- 1 egg
- Salt and pepper to taste
- 1 cup pineapple juice
- 1/2 cup brown sugar
- 1/2 cup vinegar
- 1/4 cup soy sauce
- 1 tablespoon cornstarch mixed with 2 tablespoons water

Instructions:

1. **Make Meatballs:** In a bowl, combine ground beef, breadcrumbs, onion, egg, salt, and pepper. Form into 1-inch meatballs.
2. **Bake Meatballs:** Preheat oven to 375°F (190°C). Place meatballs on a baking sheet and bake for 20 minutes until cooked through.
3. **Prepare Sauce:** In a saucepan, combine pineapple juice, brown sugar, vinegar, and soy sauce. Bring to a boil, then reduce heat. Stir in cornstarch mixture to thicken.
4. **Combine:** Add cooked meatballs to the sauce, simmering for 5 minutes.
5. **Serve:** Serve meatballs with sauce over rice or noodles.

Slow Cooker Ribs with Barbecue Sauce

Ingredients:

- 2 pounds baby back ribs
- 1 cup barbecue sauce
- 1/4 cup apple cider vinegar
- 1 tablespoon brown sugar
- 1 tablespoon garlic powder
- 1 tablespoon onion powder
- Salt and pepper to taste

Instructions:

1. **Prepare Ribs:** Remove the membrane from the ribs and season with salt, pepper, garlic powder, and onion powder.
2. **Mix Sauce:** In a bowl, combine barbecue sauce, apple cider vinegar, and brown sugar.
3. **Slow Cook:** Place ribs in a slow cooker and pour the sauce mixture over them. Cook on low for 6-8 hours or until tender.
4. **Serve:** Remove ribs from the slow cooker and serve with additional barbecue sauce.

Chicken and Dumplings

Ingredients:

- 1 pound boneless, skinless chicken thighs, diced
- 4 cups chicken broth
- 1 cup carrots, diced
- 1 cup celery, diced
- 1 onion, chopped
- 2 cups biscuit mix
- 3/4 cup milk
- Salt and pepper to taste
- 1 teaspoon thyme
- 1 teaspoon parsley

Instructions:

1. **Cook Chicken:** In a large pot, combine chicken, chicken broth, carrots, celery, onion, thyme, salt, and pepper. Bring to a boil, then simmer until chicken is cooked.
2. **Make Dumplings:** In a bowl, mix biscuit mix and milk until combined.
3. **Add Dumplings:** Drop spoonfuls of the dumpling mixture into the simmering broth. Cover and cook for 15-20 minutes until dumplings are cooked through.
4. **Serve:** Garnish with parsley and serve hot.

Beef Stroganoff

Ingredients:

- 1 pound beef sirloin, sliced thinly
- 1 onion, chopped
- 2 cups mushrooms, sliced
- 2 cloves garlic, minced
- 1 cup beef broth
- 1 cup sour cream
- 2 tablespoons flour
- 2 tablespoons olive oil
- Salt and pepper to taste
- Cooked egg noodles for serving

Instructions:

1. **Sauté Beef:** In a skillet, heat olive oil over medium-high heat. Add beef, cooking until browned. Remove and set aside.
2. **Cook Vegetables:** In the same skillet, add onion, garlic, and mushrooms. Cook until softened.
3. **Make Sauce:** Sprinkle flour over the vegetables, stirring to coat. Slowly add beef broth, stirring until thickened. Remove from heat and stir in sour cream.
4. **Combine:** Return beef to the skillet, stirring to combine. Heat through.
5. **Serve:** Serve over cooked egg noodles.

Mediterranean Chickpea Stew

Ingredients:

- 1 tablespoon olive oil
- 1 onion, chopped
- 2 cloves garlic, minced
- 1 can (15 oz) chickpeas, drained and rinsed
- 1 can (14.5 oz) diced tomatoes
- 1 cup vegetable broth
- 1 teaspoon cumin
- 1 teaspoon paprika
- 1 teaspoon oregano
- Salt and pepper to taste
- Fresh parsley for garnish

Instructions:

1. **Sauté Onions and Garlic:** In a large pot, heat olive oil over medium heat. Add onion and garlic, cooking until softened.
2. **Add Remaining Ingredients:** Stir in chickpeas, diced tomatoes, vegetable broth, cumin, paprika, oregano, salt, and pepper.
3. **Simmer:** Bring to a boil, then reduce heat and simmer for 20-30 minutes.
4. **Serve:** Garnish with fresh parsley and serve hot.

Classic Beef Chili

Ingredients:

- 1 pound ground beef
- 1 onion, chopped
- 2 cloves garlic, minced
- 1 can (15 oz) kidney beans, drained and rinsed
- 1 can (15 oz) diced tomatoes
- 1 cup beef broth
- 2 tablespoons chili powder
- 1 teaspoon cumin
- Salt and pepper to taste

Instructions:

1. **Cook Beef:** In a large pot, cook ground beef over medium heat until browned. Drain excess fat.
2. **Add Vegetables:** Stir in onion and garlic, cooking until softened.
3. **Add Remaining Ingredients:** Add kidney beans, diced tomatoes, beef broth, chili powder, cumin, salt, and pepper. Bring to a boil.
4. **Simmer:** Reduce heat and simmer for 30-40 minutes.
5. **Serve:** Serve hot with your choice of toppings.

Teriyaki Chicken with Pineapple

Ingredients:

- 1 pound boneless, skinless chicken thighs, diced
- 1 cup pineapple chunks (fresh or canned)
- 1/2 cup soy sauce
- 1/4 cup brown sugar
- 2 tablespoons rice vinegar
- 2 cloves garlic, minced
- 1 tablespoon cornstarch mixed with 2 tablespoons water
- Sesame seeds for garnish
- Cooked rice for serving

Instructions:

1. **Prepare Sauce:** In a bowl, mix soy sauce, brown sugar, rice vinegar, and garlic.
2. **Cook Chicken:** In a skillet, cook diced chicken over medium heat until browned.
3. **Add Pineapple and Sauce:** Stir in pineapple and teriyaki sauce. Bring to a simmer.
4. **Thicken Sauce:** Add cornstarch mixture, stirring until thickened.
5. **Serve:** Serve over cooked rice and garnish with sesame seeds.

Enjoy these delicious and comforting recipes!

Savory Pot Roast with Potatoes

Ingredients:

- 3 to 4 pounds chuck roast
- 2 tablespoons olive oil
- Salt and pepper to taste
- 4 carrots, chopped
- 4 potatoes, quartered
- 1 onion, quartered
- 3 cloves garlic, minced
- 1 cup beef broth
- 2 tablespoons Worcestershire sauce
- 2 teaspoons dried thyme
- 2 bay leaves

Instructions:

1. **Sear the Meat:** Preheat oven to 325°F (160°C). In a large Dutch oven, heat olive oil over medium-high heat. Season the chuck roast with salt and pepper. Sear the roast on all sides until browned.
2. **Add Vegetables:** Remove the roast and set aside. Add carrots, potatoes, onion, and garlic to the pot, sautéing for a few minutes.
3. **Deglaze and Cook:** Return the roast to the pot. Add beef broth, Worcestershire sauce, thyme, and bay leaves. Bring to a simmer.
4. **Roast:** Cover and transfer to the oven. Cook for 3-4 hours or until the meat is tender and easily shredded.
5. **Serve:** Remove the bay leaves, slice the roast, and serve with the vegetables.

Lemon Garlic Herb Chicken

Ingredients:

- 4 bone-in chicken thighs
- 2 tablespoons olive oil
- 4 cloves garlic, minced
- Juice of 1 lemon
- 1 tablespoon fresh rosemary, chopped
- 1 tablespoon fresh thyme, chopped
- Salt and pepper to taste

Instructions:

1. **Marinate Chicken:** In a bowl, combine olive oil, garlic, lemon juice, rosemary, thyme, salt, and pepper. Add chicken thighs, coating well. Marinate for at least 30 minutes.
2. **Preheat Oven:** Preheat the oven to 400°F (200°C).
3. **Bake Chicken:** Place chicken in a baking dish and pour any remaining marinade over the top. Bake for 35-40 minutes or until the chicken is cooked through and golden.
4. **Serve:** Let rest for a few minutes before serving.

Stuffed Bell Peppers

Ingredients:

- 4 large bell peppers (any color)
- 1 pound ground beef or turkey
- 1 cup cooked rice
- 1 can (15 oz) diced tomatoes
- 1 teaspoon Italian seasoning
- Salt and pepper to taste
- 1 cup shredded cheese (cheddar or mozzarella)

Instructions:

1. **Prepare Peppers:** Preheat oven to 375°F (190°C). Cut the tops off the bell peppers and remove seeds.
2. **Make Filling:** In a skillet, brown the ground meat. Add cooked rice, diced tomatoes, Italian seasoning, salt, and pepper. Mix well.
3. **Stuff Peppers:** Fill each bell pepper with the meat mixture and place in a baking dish. Top with shredded cheese.
4. **Bake:** Cover with foil and bake for 30 minutes. Remove foil and bake for an additional 10 minutes until cheese is melted.
5. **Serve:** Let cool slightly before serving.

Beef and Mushroom Stroganoff

Ingredients:

- 1 pound beef sirloin, sliced thinly
- 1 cup mushrooms, sliced
- 1 onion, chopped
- 2 cloves garlic, minced
- 1 cup beef broth
- 1 cup sour cream
- 2 tablespoons flour
- 2 tablespoons olive oil
- Salt and pepper to taste
- Cooked egg noodles for serving

Instructions:

1. **Cook Beef:** In a skillet, heat olive oil over medium-high heat. Add sliced beef, cooking until browned. Remove and set aside.
2. **Sauté Vegetables:** In the same skillet, add onion, garlic, and mushrooms, cooking until softened.
3. **Make Sauce:** Sprinkle flour over the vegetables and stir to combine. Gradually add beef broth, stirring until thickened. Remove from heat and stir in sour cream.
4. **Combine:** Return beef to the skillet and stir to coat in the sauce.
5. **Serve:** Serve over cooked egg noodles.

Thai Red Curry with Chicken

Ingredients:

- 1 pound boneless, skinless chicken thighs, sliced
- 1 can (14 oz) coconut milk
- 2 tablespoons red curry paste
- 1 tablespoon fish sauce
- 1 tablespoon brown sugar
- 1 red bell pepper, sliced
- 1 cup snap peas
- Fresh basil for garnish
- Cooked jasmine rice for serving

Instructions:

1. **Cook Chicken:** In a large skillet, heat coconut milk over medium heat. Add red curry paste, stirring until combined. Add sliced chicken and cook until no longer pink.
2. **Add Vegetables:** Stir in fish sauce, brown sugar, bell pepper, and snap peas. Simmer for 5-7 minutes until vegetables are tender.
3. **Serve:** Serve over jasmine rice and garnish with fresh basil.

Moroccan Lamb Tagine

Ingredients:

- 2 pounds lamb shoulder, cubed
- 1 onion, chopped
- 3 cloves garlic, minced
- 1 can (14 oz) diced tomatoes
- 2 cups vegetable broth
- 1/2 cup dried apricots, chopped
- 2 tablespoons Moroccan spice blend (cumin, coriander, cinnamon, ginger)
- Salt and pepper to taste
- Fresh cilantro for garnish

Instructions:

1. **Brown Lamb:** In a large pot, brown lamb cubes over medium-high heat. Remove and set aside.
2. **Sauté Onions and Garlic:** In the same pot, add onions and garlic, cooking until softened.
3. **Combine Ingredients:** Return lamb to the pot, adding diced tomatoes, vegetable broth, dried apricots, Moroccan spices, salt, and pepper.
4. **Simmer:** Bring to a boil, then reduce heat and simmer for 1.5-2 hours until lamb is tender.
5. **Serve:** Garnish with fresh cilantro and serve with couscous or bread.

Chicken Enchilada Casserole

Ingredients:

- 2 cups cooked shredded chicken
- 1 can (10 oz) enchilada sauce
- 1 can (15 oz) black beans, drained and rinsed
- 1 cup corn kernels
- 2 cups shredded cheese (cheddar or Mexican blend)
- 8 corn tortillas, cut into strips
- 1 teaspoon cumin
- Salt and pepper to taste
- Fresh cilantro for garnish

Instructions:

1. **Preheat Oven:** Preheat oven to 350°F (175°C).
2. **Layer Ingredients:** In a baking dish, layer half of the tortillas, followed by half of the chicken, black beans, corn, enchilada sauce, and cheese. Repeat layers.
3. **Bake:** Cover with foil and bake for 25-30 minutes. Remove foil and bake for an additional 10-15 minutes until cheese is bubbly.
4. **Serve:** Garnish with fresh cilantro and serve hot.

Lentil and Spinach Soup

Ingredients:

- 1 tablespoon olive oil
- 1 onion, chopped
- 2 carrots, diced
- 2 celery stalks, diced
- 2 cloves garlic, minced
- 1 cup lentils, rinsed
- 6 cups vegetable broth
- 1 teaspoon cumin
- Salt and pepper to taste
- 4 cups fresh spinach
- Lemon wedges for serving

Instructions:

1. **Sauté Vegetables:** In a large pot, heat olive oil over medium heat. Add onion, carrots, and celery, cooking until softened. Stir in garlic and cook for another minute.
2. **Add Lentils and Broth:** Add lentils, vegetable broth, cumin, salt, and pepper. Bring to a boil, then reduce heat and simmer for 30-40 minutes until lentils are tender.
3. **Add Spinach:** Stir in fresh spinach and cook until wilted.
4. **Serve:** Serve hot with lemon wedges on the side.

Enjoy these hearty and flavorful recipes!

Garlic Parmesan Chicken Wings

Ingredients:

- 2 pounds chicken wings
- 1/2 cup unsalted butter, melted
- 4 cloves garlic, minced
- 1/2 cup grated Parmesan cheese
- 1 tablespoon chopped fresh parsley
- Salt and pepper to taste
- Optional: 1/2 teaspoon red pepper flakes for heat

Instructions:

1. **Preheat Oven:** Preheat the oven to 400°F (200°C). Line a baking sheet with foil and place a wire rack on top.
2. **Prepare Wings:** Pat the chicken wings dry with paper towels. Season with salt and pepper, then arrange in a single layer on the wire rack.
3. **Bake:** Bake wings for 40-45 minutes, turning halfway, until crispy and golden.
4. **Make Sauce:** While wings are baking, combine melted butter, garlic, Parmesan cheese, parsley, and red pepper flakes in a bowl.
5. **Coat and Serve:** Toss baked wings in the garlic Parmesan sauce and serve immediately.

BBQ Brisket

Ingredients:

- 4-5 pounds beef brisket
- 1 tablespoon paprika
- 1 tablespoon brown sugar
- 1 tablespoon garlic powder
- 1 tablespoon onion powder
- 1 teaspoon black pepper
- 1 teaspoon salt
- 1 cup beef broth
- 1 cup BBQ sauce

Instructions:

1. **Preheat Oven:** Preheat the oven to 300°F (150°C).
2. **Season Brisket:** In a small bowl, combine paprika, brown sugar, garlic powder, onion powder, black pepper, and salt. Rub the spice mixture all over the brisket.
3. **Bake:** Place the brisket in a roasting pan and pour beef broth around it. Cover tightly with foil and bake for 4-5 hours, or until fork-tender.
4. **Glaze:** Remove from the oven, brush with BBQ sauce, and return to the oven uncovered for an additional 30 minutes.
5. **Serve:** Slice against the grain and serve with extra BBQ sauce.

Curried Lentil Stew

Ingredients:

- 1 tablespoon olive oil
- 1 onion, chopped
- 2 carrots, diced
- 2 cloves garlic, minced
- 1 tablespoon curry powder
- 1 teaspoon cumin
- 1 cup lentils (green or brown), rinsed
- 4 cups vegetable broth
- 1 can (14 oz) diced tomatoes
- 2 cups spinach
- Salt and pepper to taste

Instructions:

1. **Sauté Vegetables:** In a large pot, heat olive oil over medium heat. Add onion, carrots, and garlic, cooking until softened.
2. **Add Spices:** Stir in curry powder and cumin, cooking for another minute until fragrant.
3. **Add Lentils and Broth:** Add lentils, vegetable broth, and diced tomatoes. Bring to a boil, then reduce heat and simmer for 30-35 minutes until lentils are tender.
4. **Add Spinach:** Stir in spinach and cook until wilted. Season with salt and pepper to taste.
5. **Serve:** Serve hot with crusty bread.

Shrimp and Grits

Ingredients:

- 1 cup grits (quick-cooking)
- 4 cups chicken broth
- 1 pound shrimp, peeled and deveined
- 4 slices bacon, chopped
- 1/2 cup heavy cream
- 1 tablespoon Worcestershire sauce
- 2 cloves garlic, minced
- 1 teaspoon paprika
- Salt and pepper to taste
- Chopped green onions for garnish

Instructions:

1. **Cook Grits:** In a saucepan, bring chicken broth to a boil. Stir in grits and reduce heat to low, cooking until thickened (about 5-7 minutes). Stir in heavy cream and season with salt and pepper.
2. **Cook Bacon:** In a large skillet, cook bacon over medium heat until crispy. Remove bacon and set aside, leaving drippings in the pan.
3. **Sauté Shrimp:** Add garlic to the skillet, cooking until fragrant. Add shrimp, Worcestershire sauce, paprika, salt, and pepper. Cook until shrimp are pink and cooked through (about 3-4 minutes).
4. **Serve:** Serve shrimp over grits, topped with bacon and green onions.

Chicken Fajitas

Ingredients:

- 1 pound boneless, skinless chicken breasts, sliced
- 1 tablespoon olive oil
- 1 teaspoon chili powder
- 1 teaspoon cumin
- 1/2 teaspoon paprika
- 1 bell pepper, sliced
- 1 onion, sliced
- Salt and pepper to taste
- Flour or corn tortillas for serving
- Optional toppings: sour cream, guacamole, salsa

Instructions:

1. **Season Chicken:** In a bowl, combine chicken, olive oil, chili powder, cumin, paprika, salt, and pepper. Mix until chicken is coated.
2. **Cook Chicken:** Heat a skillet over medium-high heat. Add seasoned chicken and cook until browned and cooked through (about 6-7 minutes). Remove and set aside.
3. **Sauté Vegetables:** In the same skillet, add bell pepper and onion, cooking until softened.
4. **Combine:** Return chicken to the skillet, stirring to combine. Cook for another minute.
5. **Serve:** Serve in tortillas with desired toppings.

Italian Sausage and Peppers

Ingredients:

- 1 pound Italian sausage (mild or hot)
- 1 onion, sliced
- 2 bell peppers, sliced
- 3 cloves garlic, minced
- 1 can (14 oz) diced tomatoes
- 1 teaspoon Italian seasoning
- Salt and pepper to taste
- Crusty bread or hoagie rolls for serving

Instructions:

1. **Brown Sausage:** In a large skillet, brown Italian sausage over medium heat. Remove and slice into pieces.
2. **Sauté Vegetables:** In the same skillet, add onion and bell peppers, cooking until softened. Add garlic and cook for an additional minute.
3. **Add Sausage and Tomatoes:** Return sausage to the skillet, adding diced tomatoes and Italian seasoning. Simmer for 10-15 minutes.
4. **Serve:** Serve hot on crusty bread or in hoagie rolls.

Chicken and Rice Casserole

Ingredients:

- 2 cups cooked chicken, shredded
- 1 cup uncooked rice
- 2 cups chicken broth
- 1 can (10.5 oz) cream of chicken soup
- 1 cup frozen mixed vegetables
- 1 teaspoon garlic powder
- Salt and pepper to taste
- 1 cup shredded cheese (cheddar or mozzarella)

Instructions:

1. **Preheat Oven:** Preheat oven to 350°F (175°C).
2. **Combine Ingredients:** In a large bowl, mix cooked chicken, uncooked rice, chicken broth, cream of chicken soup, mixed vegetables, garlic powder, salt, and pepper.
3. **Bake:** Pour the mixture into a greased casserole dish. Cover with foil and bake for 45 minutes. Remove foil, top with cheese, and bake for an additional 10-15 minutes until cheese is melted and bubbly.
4. **Serve:** Let cool for a few minutes before serving.

Classic French Onion Soup

Ingredients:

- 4 large onions, thinly sliced
- 4 tablespoons butter
- 1 teaspoon sugar
- 4 cups beef broth
- 1 cup white wine (optional)
- 1 tablespoon thyme
- Salt and pepper to taste
- Baguette slices
- 1 cup shredded Gruyère cheese

Instructions:

1. **Caramelize Onions:** In a large pot, melt butter over medium heat. Add sliced onions and sugar, cooking until caramelized (about 20-30 minutes).
2. **Add Broth and Wine:** Stir in beef broth, white wine, thyme, salt, and pepper. Bring to a simmer and cook for 20 minutes.
3. **Prepare Bread:** Preheat broiler. Place baguette slices on a baking sheet, top with cheese, and broil until bubbly and golden.
4. **Serve:** Ladle soup into bowls, top with cheesy bread, and serve hot.

Enjoy these delicious recipes!

Jambalaya with Chicken and Sausage

Ingredients:

- 1 pound andouille sausage, sliced
- 1 pound chicken thighs, diced
- 1 onion, chopped
- 1 bell pepper, chopped
- 2 celery stalks, chopped
- 3 cloves garlic, minced
- 1 can (14.5 oz) diced tomatoes
- 2 cups chicken broth
- 1 tablespoon Cajun seasoning
- 1 cup long-grain rice
- 1 bay leaf
- Salt and pepper to taste
- 1 cup green onions, sliced (for garnish)
- Optional: 1 pound shrimp, peeled and deveined

Instructions:

1. **Cook Sausage and Chicken:** In a large pot, cook the sausage over medium heat until browned. Add the chicken and cook until browned and cooked through. Remove from the pot and set aside.
2. **Sauté Vegetables:** In the same pot, add onion, bell pepper, celery, and garlic. Cook until softened.
3. **Add Ingredients:** Stir in diced tomatoes, chicken broth, Cajun seasoning, rice, bay leaf, salt, and pepper. Bring to a boil.
4. **Simmer:** Reduce heat to low, cover, and simmer for about 20 minutes. If using shrimp, add them in the last 5 minutes of cooking.
5. **Serve:** Remove the bay leaf, fluff with a fork, and garnish with green onions before serving.

Beef and Vegetable Stir-Fry

Ingredients:

- 1 pound beef (flank steak or sirloin), thinly sliced
- 2 tablespoons soy sauce
- 1 tablespoon cornstarch
- 2 tablespoons vegetable oil
- 1 bell pepper, sliced
- 1 cup broccoli florets
- 1 cup snap peas
- 2 carrots, sliced
- 3 cloves garlic, minced
- 1 tablespoon ginger, minced
- 1/4 cup beef broth
- Optional: Cooked rice for serving

Instructions:

1. **Marinate Beef:** In a bowl, combine beef, soy sauce, and cornstarch. Let marinate for 15-30 minutes.
2. **Stir-Fry Beef:** Heat 1 tablespoon of oil in a large skillet or wok over high heat. Add beef and stir-fry until browned. Remove and set aside.
3. **Cook Vegetables:** In the same skillet, add remaining oil and stir-fry bell pepper, broccoli, snap peas, and carrots for about 5 minutes. Add garlic and ginger, cooking for an additional minute.
4. **Combine:** Return beef to the skillet, add beef broth, and stir until heated through.
5. **Serve:** Serve hot over cooked rice, if desired.

Creamy Mushroom Chicken

Ingredients:

- 4 boneless, skinless chicken breasts
- 2 cups mushrooms, sliced
- 1 onion, chopped
- 3 cloves garlic, minced
- 1 cup heavy cream
- 1 cup chicken broth
- 1 tablespoon olive oil
- 1 teaspoon thyme
- Salt and pepper to taste
- Fresh parsley for garnish

Instructions:

1. **Cook Chicken:** In a skillet, heat olive oil over medium heat. Season chicken with salt and pepper, then cook until golden and cooked through (about 6-7 minutes per side). Remove and set aside.
2. **Sauté Vegetables:** In the same skillet, add onions and mushrooms, cooking until softened. Add garlic and thyme, cooking for another minute.
3. **Make Sauce:** Stir in chicken broth and heavy cream, bringing to a simmer. Cook until slightly thickened.
4. **Combine:** Return chicken to the skillet, spooning sauce over it. Cook for a few more minutes until heated through.
5. **Serve:** Garnish with fresh parsley before serving.

Stuffed Cabbage Rolls

Ingredients:

- 1 large head of cabbage
- 1 pound ground beef
- 1 cup cooked rice
- 1 onion, chopped
- 1 egg
- 1 can (15 oz) tomato sauce
- 1 tablespoon Worcestershire sauce
- Salt and pepper to taste
- 2 cups beef broth
- Optional: Additional tomato sauce for topping

Instructions:

1. **Prepare Cabbage:** Bring a large pot of water to a boil. Carefully remove cabbage leaves, blanch them in boiling water for 2-3 minutes until softened, and set aside.
2. **Make Filling:** In a bowl, combine ground beef, cooked rice, onion, egg, Worcestershire sauce, salt, and pepper.
3. **Stuff Rolls:** Place a portion of filling on each cabbage leaf, rolling tightly and tucking in the sides. Secure with toothpicks if needed.
4. **Cook:** In a large pot, layer stuffed cabbage rolls, pour beef broth and tomato sauce over the top, and simmer for about 45 minutes.
5. **Serve:** Remove toothpicks, and serve warm with additional tomato sauce if desired.

Spanish Chicken and Rice

Ingredients:

- 1 pound chicken thighs, bone-in and skin-on
- 1 onion, chopped
- 1 bell pepper, chopped
- 2 cloves garlic, minced
- 1 can (14.5 oz) diced tomatoes
- 2 cups chicken broth
- 1 cup long-grain rice
- 1 teaspoon smoked paprika
- 1/2 teaspoon saffron (optional)
- 1 cup frozen peas
- Salt and pepper to taste

Instructions:

1. **Brown Chicken:** In a large skillet, brown chicken thighs over medium heat on both sides. Remove and set aside.
2. **Sauté Vegetables:** In the same skillet, add onion, bell pepper, and garlic, cooking until softened.
3. **Add Rice and Liquid:** Stir in rice, diced tomatoes, chicken broth, smoked paprika, saffron (if using), salt, and pepper. Bring to a boil.
4. **Cook Chicken:** Return chicken to the skillet, cover, and reduce heat to low. Simmer for 25-30 minutes until rice is cooked and chicken is tender.
5. **Add Peas:** Stir in frozen peas in the last 5 minutes of cooking. Serve hot.

Italian Meatball Soup

Ingredients:

- 1 pound ground beef or turkey
- 1/2 cup breadcrumbs
- 1/4 cup grated Parmesan cheese
- 1 egg
- 2 cloves garlic, minced
- 1 teaspoon Italian seasoning
- Salt and pepper to taste
- 6 cups chicken broth
- 1 can (14.5 oz) diced tomatoes
- 2 cups spinach or kale
- Optional: Cooked pasta for serving

Instructions:

1. **Make Meatballs:** In a bowl, combine ground meat, breadcrumbs, Parmesan, egg, garlic, Italian seasoning, salt, and pepper. Form into small meatballs.
2. **Cook Meatballs:** In a large pot, bring chicken broth to a simmer. Carefully add meatballs and cook until they are cooked through (about 10-12 minutes).
3. **Add Tomatoes and Greens:** Stir in diced tomatoes and spinach. Cook for an additional 5 minutes until spinach is wilted.
4. **Serve:** Serve hot, optionally adding cooked pasta.

Zesty Ranch Chicken

Ingredients:

- 4 boneless, skinless chicken breasts
- 1 packet ranch seasoning mix
- 1/2 cup plain Greek yogurt
- 1/4 cup mayonnaise
- 1 tablespoon lemon juice
- 1 tablespoon olive oil
- Salt and pepper to taste
- Optional: Chopped fresh herbs for garnish

Instructions:

1. **Preheat Oven:** Preheat oven to 375°F (190°C).
2. **Prepare Marinade:** In a bowl, combine ranch seasoning, Greek yogurt, mayonnaise, lemon juice, olive oil, salt, and pepper.
3. **Marinate Chicken:** Coat chicken breasts with the marinade, placing them in a baking dish.
4. **Bake:** Bake for 25-30 minutes until chicken is cooked through and reaches an internal temperature of 165°F (75°C).
5. **Serve:** Garnish with fresh herbs and serve hot.

Vegetable and Quinoa Chili

Ingredients:

- 1 tablespoon olive oil
- 1 onion, chopped
- 2 cloves garlic, minced
- 1 bell pepper, chopped
- 2 carrots, diced
- 1 zucchini, diced
- 1 can (14.5 oz) diced tomatoes
- 1 can (15 oz) black beans, drained and rinsed
- 1 cup vegetable broth
- 1 cup quinoa, rinsed
- 1 tablespoon chili powder
- 1 teaspoon cumin
- Salt and pepper to taste
- Optional: Avocado and cilantro for garnish

Instructions:

1. **Sauté Vegetables:** In a large pot, heat olive oil over medium heat. Add onion and garlic, cooking until softened. Add bell pepper, carrots, and zucchini, cooking for about 5 minutes.
2. **Add Remaining Ingredients:** Stir in diced tomatoes, black beans, vegetable broth, quinoa, chili powder, cumin, salt, and pepper. Bring to a boil.
3. **Simmer:** Reduce heat and simmer for about 20 minutes, or until quinoa is cooked and vegetables are tender.
4. **Serve:** Garnish with avocado and cilantro before serving.

Feel free to adjust the seasonings and ingredients based on your preferences!

Coconut Curry Chicken

Ingredients:

- 1 pound chicken thighs, boneless and skinless, cut into chunks
- 1 onion, chopped
- 2 cloves garlic, minced
- 1 tablespoon ginger, minced
- 1 can (14 oz) coconut milk
- 2 tablespoons red curry paste
- 1 bell pepper, sliced
- 1 cup broccoli florets
- 2 tablespoons fish sauce
- 1 tablespoon brown sugar
- 2 tablespoons vegetable oil
- Fresh cilantro for garnish
- Cooked rice for serving

Instructions:

1. **Sauté Aromatics:** Heat vegetable oil in a large skillet over medium heat. Add onion, garlic, and ginger, sautéing until fragrant.
2. **Cook Chicken:** Add chicken to the skillet, cooking until browned on all sides.
3. **Add Curry Paste:** Stir in red curry paste, cooking for 1-2 minutes until well combined.
4. **Add Coconut Milk and Veggies:** Pour in coconut milk, fish sauce, and brown sugar. Add bell pepper and broccoli, stirring to combine.
5. **Simmer:** Bring to a simmer and cook for 15-20 minutes until chicken is cooked through and vegetables are tender.
6. **Serve:** Garnish with fresh cilantro and serve over cooked rice.

Pork Carnitas

Ingredients:

- 2 pounds pork shoulder, cut into large chunks
- 1 onion, quartered
- 4 cloves garlic, minced
- 1 tablespoon cumin
- 1 tablespoon chili powder
- 1 teaspoon oregano
- 1 teaspoon salt
- 1/2 teaspoon black pepper
- 1/2 cup orange juice
- 1 lime, juiced
- 2 bay leaves
- Fresh cilantro for garnish
- Tortillas for serving

Instructions:

1. **Season Pork:** In a slow cooker, combine pork chunks with onion, garlic, cumin, chili powder, oregano, salt, and pepper.
2. **Add Liquid:** Pour in orange juice and lime juice, adding bay leaves on top.
3. **Cook:** Cover and cook on low for 8-10 hours, or until pork is tender and easily shredded.
4. **Shred Meat:** Remove pork from the slow cooker, shred it with forks, and return it to the juices to soak up the flavor.
5. **Serve:** Garnish with fresh cilantro and serve with tortillas.

Chicken Cacciatore

Ingredients:

- 4 boneless, skinless chicken breasts
- 1 onion, sliced
- 1 bell pepper, sliced
- 2 cloves garlic, minced
- 1 can (14.5 oz) diced tomatoes
- 1 cup chicken broth
- 1 teaspoon dried oregano
- 1 teaspoon dried basil
- Salt and pepper to taste
- 2 tablespoons olive oil
- Fresh parsley for garnish

Instructions:

1. **Brown Chicken:** In a large skillet, heat olive oil over medium heat. Season chicken with salt and pepper, then brown on both sides. Remove and set aside.
2. **Sauté Vegetables:** In the same skillet, add onion, bell pepper, and garlic, cooking until softened.
3. **Add Tomatoes and Broth:** Stir in diced tomatoes, chicken broth, oregano, and basil. Return chicken to the skillet.
4. **Simmer:** Cover and simmer for 30 minutes until chicken is cooked through.
5. **Serve:** Garnish with fresh parsley before serving.

BBQ Chicken Thighs

Ingredients:

- 4 chicken thighs, bone-in and skin-on
- 1 cup BBQ sauce
- 1 tablespoon olive oil
- 1 teaspoon garlic powder
- 1 teaspoon paprika
- Salt and pepper to taste

Instructions:

1. **Preheat Oven:** Preheat oven to 375°F (190°C).
2. **Season Chicken:** In a bowl, mix BBQ sauce, olive oil, garlic powder, paprika, salt, and pepper. Coat chicken thighs with the mixture.
3. **Bake:** Place chicken in a baking dish and bake for 35-40 minutes until cooked through and juices run clear.
4. **Serve:** Serve with extra BBQ sauce if desired.

Beef Bourguignon

Ingredients:

- 2 pounds beef chuck, cut into 1-inch cubes
- 4 slices bacon, chopped
- 1 onion, chopped
- 2 carrots, sliced
- 2 cloves garlic, minced
- 1 bottle (750 ml) red wine (Burgundy recommended)
- 2 cups beef broth
- 2 tablespoons tomato paste
- 1 teaspoon thyme
- 2 bay leaves
- Salt and pepper to taste
- Fresh parsley for garnish

Instructions:

1. **Cook Bacon:** In a large pot, cook bacon over medium heat until crispy. Remove and set aside.
2. **Brown Beef:** In the bacon fat, brown the beef cubes in batches, then remove and set aside.
3. **Sauté Vegetables:** Add onion and carrots to the pot, cooking until softened. Stir in garlic and cook for 1 minute.
4. **Add Liquids and Beef:** Return beef and bacon to the pot. Stir in wine, beef broth, tomato paste, thyme, bay leaves, salt, and pepper.
5. **Simmer:** Bring to a simmer, cover, and cook for 2-3 hours until beef is tender.
6. **Serve:** Remove bay leaves and garnish with fresh parsley before serving.

Chicken Tortilla Soup

Ingredients:

- 1 pound chicken breasts, cooked and shredded
- 1 onion, chopped
- 2 cloves garlic, minced
- 1 can (14.5 oz) diced tomatoes
- 4 cups chicken broth
- 1 teaspoon cumin
- 1 teaspoon chili powder
- 1 can (15 oz) black beans, drained and rinsed
- 1 cup corn (fresh or frozen)
- Salt and pepper to taste
- Tortilla strips for serving
- Optional: Avocado, cilantro, cheese for garnish

Instructions:

1. **Sauté Vegetables:** In a large pot, sauté onion and garlic over medium heat until softened.
2. **Add Ingredients:** Stir in diced tomatoes, chicken broth, cumin, chili powder, black beans, corn, salt, and pepper.
3. **Simmer:** Bring to a simmer and cook for 15 minutes. Add shredded chicken and heat through.
4. **Serve:** Serve hot, garnished with tortilla strips and optional toppings.

Tomato and Basil Risotto

Ingredients:

- 1 cup Arborio rice
- 4 cups chicken or vegetable broth
- 1 onion, chopped
- 2 cloves garlic, minced
- 1 can (14.5 oz) diced tomatoes, drained
- 1 cup fresh basil, chopped
- 1/2 cup grated Parmesan cheese
- 2 tablespoons olive oil
- Salt and pepper to taste

Instructions:

1. **Sauté Aromatics:** In a large pot, heat olive oil over medium heat. Add onion and garlic, cooking until softened.
2. **Add Rice:** Stir in Arborio rice and cook for 1-2 minutes until slightly toasted.
3. **Add Broth Gradually:** Add broth one cup at a time, stirring constantly and allowing the rice to absorb the liquid before adding more.
4. **Add Tomatoes and Basil:** After about 20 minutes, stir in diced tomatoes and fresh basil, cooking until the rice is creamy and al dente.
5. **Finish:** Remove from heat, stir in Parmesan cheese, and season with salt and pepper before serving.

Enjoy these delicious recipes! Feel free to customize any of them to suit your taste preferences!

Beef and Barley Soup

Ingredients:

- 1 pound beef stew meat, cut into cubes
- 1 tablespoon olive oil
- 1 onion, chopped
- 2 carrots, sliced
- 2 celery stalks, chopped
- 2 cloves garlic, minced
- 6 cups beef broth
- 1 cup pearl barley, rinsed
- 1 can (14.5 oz) diced tomatoes
- 1 teaspoon dried thyme
- 2 bay leaves
- Salt and pepper to taste
- Fresh parsley for garnish

Instructions:

1. **Brown the Meat:** In a large pot, heat olive oil over medium heat. Add beef stew meat and brown on all sides. Remove and set aside.
2. **Sauté Vegetables:** In the same pot, add onion, carrots, and celery. Sauté until softened, about 5-7 minutes. Stir in garlic and cook for 1 more minute.
3. **Add Ingredients:** Return the beef to the pot and add beef broth, pearl barley, diced tomatoes, thyme, bay leaves, salt, and pepper.
4. **Simmer:** Bring to a boil, then reduce heat and simmer for about 1 hour, or until the barley is tender and the beef is cooked through.
5. **Serve:** Remove bay leaves, garnish with fresh parsley, and serve hot.

Italian Sausage and Lentil Soup

Ingredients:

- 1 pound Italian sausage, casings removed
- 1 onion, chopped
- 2 carrots, diced
- 2 celery stalks, diced
- 2 cloves garlic, minced
- 1 cup dried lentils, rinsed
- 6 cups chicken or vegetable broth
- 1 can (14.5 oz) diced tomatoes
- 1 teaspoon dried oregano
- 1 teaspoon dried basil
- Salt and pepper to taste
- Fresh spinach (optional)

Instructions:

1. **Brown the Sausage:** In a large pot, cook the Italian sausage over medium heat until browned. Break it into crumbles as it cooks. Remove and set aside.
2. **Sauté Vegetables:** In the same pot, add onion, carrots, and celery. Sauté until softened, about 5-7 minutes. Stir in garlic and cook for 1 more minute.
3. **Add Remaining Ingredients:** Add lentils, broth, diced tomatoes, oregano, basil, salt, and pepper to the pot. Return the sausage to the pot.
4. **Simmer:** Bring to a boil, then reduce heat and simmer for about 30-40 minutes until lentils are tender.
5. **Optional Addition:** Stir in fresh spinach just before serving until wilted.
6. **Serve:** Ladle soup into bowls and enjoy!

Chicken Parmesan Pasta

Ingredients:

- 8 ounces pasta (spaghetti or penne)
- 2 boneless, skinless chicken breasts
- 1 cup marinara sauce
- 1 cup shredded mozzarella cheese
- 1/2 cup grated Parmesan cheese
- 1 cup breadcrumbs
- 1 teaspoon Italian seasoning
- 1 teaspoon garlic powder
- Salt and pepper to taste
- 2 tablespoons olive oil
- Fresh basil for garnish

Instructions:

1. **Cook Pasta:** Cook pasta according to package instructions. Drain and set aside.
2. **Prepare Chicken:** Preheat oven to 375°F (190°C). Season chicken breasts with salt, pepper, Italian seasoning, and garlic powder. Coat with breadcrumbs.
3. **Sear Chicken:** In a skillet, heat olive oil over medium heat. Sear the chicken on both sides until golden brown, about 4-5 minutes per side.
4. **Bake Chicken:** Transfer seared chicken to a baking dish. Top each breast with marinara sauce and shredded mozzarella. Sprinkle with grated Parmesan. Bake for 20-25 minutes or until chicken is cooked through.
5. **Combine:** Toss cooked pasta with remaining marinara sauce. Serve chicken on top of pasta.
6. **Garnish:** Garnish with fresh basil before serving.

Enjoy these comforting and delicious recipes! Let me know if you need any more!